Debt-Free

How to Get Out of Debt To Your Road Towards Financial Freedom

By

Richard Stanton

2nd Edition

Table of Contents

"Think what you do when you run in debt: you give another power over your liberty."
– Benjamin Franklin, The Way To Wealth

Introduction

This book is aimed at providing you with helpful, applicable, and relevant guidelines that you can apply directly to your regular, daily practice—guidelines that will show you how to get out of debt, and ultimately, to live a life of financial freedom.

The methods and techniques that are mentioned in this book are easy to follow and will not require you to go out of your way to incorporate them.

Each chapter in this book represents a step or a stage which is designed to teach you how to monitor your finances and make some lifestyle changes. Once you begin with following the advice in this book, it is highly suggested that you keep in mind one thing: the vision of yourself being free of debt-related commitments and being able to relax at the thought that the money flowing in and out of your life is freely coming in and freely spent, without any feelings of worry or restraint.

This vision of you is the goal that you are working at, and just like any other goal, its fulfillment requires some effort, patience, perseverance, and a lot of regular consistent practice. Thus, keep this goal in your mind, and imagine how great it would feel when you have achieved that. Let this be your motivating or driving force as you follow the steps in this book, even more so when you feel like you are struggling. Remember, any effort you take now shall remarkably pay off later on, and you can only be proud of yourself for having made a huge difference in your life now.

So, welcome to the start of your new life—one that has freedom from debt as well as the freedom to spend. Remember, each step brings you closer to that wonderful vision that you should keep in mind at all times.

Chapter 1

What Is Debt

Debt what is it? Before we can solve a problem we need to really understand what it is. The word "debt" comes from the Latin word debere, meaning to owe, taking its form from another Latin word, habere, or to have. The common definition of debt is the amount of money that is owed to financial institutions, business and individuals. It is the sum total of everything that you have borrowed from someone and is made up of both monetary and in some cases, non monetary assets. For some people it can just simply mean that Debt is the bills that are left over at the end of the month after you made the payments on everything you are able to afford. It is everything that remains back after all major payments have been made.

Let's be honest, in the long term, Debt is a destroyer of lives, families and is threat to undermine the financial security of many countries. It is often not looked as being as grave and thought as being just another expense. And what happens to be the largest form debt? It is credit card debt. In the United States, each year credit card companies earn approximately 180 billion dollars as a result of consumer debt. I am not saying that all debt is bad but Debt becomes a necessary evil when we need things that we simply can't afford. Imagine buying a huge car and using it to your heart's content but only to realize that you really cannot afford it. Will that not absolutely kill you on the inside?

In the Bible, The Book Of Proverbs 22:7, states "the borrower is the slave of the lender". Do you happen to owe 2 or more months on bills and a few thousand dollars on a few different credit cards? You must add all of your outstanding bills up and you will have the amount of your debt. If you have consumer debt especially credit card debt, then you are a slave to the credit card companies

Now that you have an understanding of what debt is. Debt factors into everyday life so easily that you don't even realize how big it is until it's too late. For yourself and your family, you must do all that you can do to get all forms of debt out of your life. Getting rid of consumer debt must be you number one number goal for yourself and your family.

The best way to achieve financial freedom or to be wealthy is to stay out of debt as much as possible. By following the steps described in the book will get you out of debt soon. It might sound like a daunting task but it needs to be done at any cost. You cannot forgo it just because it is a tough prospect. Now is the time for you to start dealing with your debts and be done with it at the earliest. And now, let us begin the process of getting out of debt by first making a List.

Chapter 2

List

This chapter talks about your first step towards becoming debt-free. This is a relatively quick step since, as suggested in the chapter's title; all you need to do is List. It may or may not take a while, depending on the length or details of your list items, but what matters is that you leave nothing out and you include anything that you find relevant. Lists have been used since time immemorial as they are easy to prepare and help people keep track of whatever is important to them. Remember to be as honest and as consistent as you can as you go through all the steps discussed in this book since doing so will help you move forward more quickly and with less difficulty when you start making the necessary financial adjustments later on.

So what do you need to make a list of? Basically, for now, you need to make a list of all the money that comes in on a monthly basis. That means you list down all the money that you acquire on a monthly basis and it can come in through any source. There can be many avenues through which you can earn your money and it need not always be only through your active income. Make sure you include your passive income as well and try and be as inclusive as possible. After that, you need to make a list of all the bills and payables that are absolutely necessary for each month. There will be more details about each list below.

Consider this whole activity of working towards a debt-free and financially free life as a major financial project of yours. Look at it at an essential part of your life and something that you need to do in order to live a happy life. Not only will you remain happy but also keep your family members happy. Hence, it would be good to have a big notebook or a folder for it, or perhaps a computer application that will help you track down everything that you write, do, or think of for this project. This will also keep everything organized for your easier reference. Use whichever works best for you and whichever you are most comfortable with and don't simply try to emulate someone else.

All throughout this book, one particular example will be used to help explain each step even further and to provide you with some kind of model or guide on how to go about each step. It is pretty much like an illustration of how lists, schedules, and ideas are made and done. You do not need to follow the exact same appearance or format. It is just used to give you a clearer idea of what to do, but you are free to create or design your own lists or templates as you deem necessary.

Now, you make your lists. As mentioned, you first make a list of all the money that regularly comes in each month. This includes your regular income from work, if any, income from any sideline jobs, any allowances, any financial aid, and so on. For example:

Monthly Income	
Company Pay	$155.00
Part-time Job	$135.00
Sales from homemade cookies	$45.00
Paid errands	$20.00
Total Income per month	$355.00

Although the amounts may have some variation, just round it off to the amount closest to the average, or perhaps to the usual lower amount that comes up. For example, your homemade cookies sales in the above list range from $45.00 to $60.00. Oftentimes, sales fall at $50.00. In any case, list down $45.00 since it is the lower amount that comes up once in a while. It is better to have some extra money later on than have to compute everything all over again because there was a budget shortage.

Your figure for paid errands above shows a relatively small amount, and for some, this may even be insignificantly small to be counted as part of the month's income, but include things like these nonetheless. Remember that small amounts can add up and turn into big amounts. This small amount of money can still cover something out of the payables you will be listing next. You need to make use of every little penny that you can earn and put it to good use.

Some people also add in money received through gift as that can also constitute passive income but since they are not regular, they need not be recorded. If you have portfolio income coming in through an investments then add in that as well. Basically, any money that is earned by you through direct or indirect means should be recorded in this column. You can choose to prepare a separate list for your spouse or add it into you list.

It will depend on how the two of you are managing your accounts. If the two of you are together contributing towards the upkeep of the house then you can add the amounts in one list but if only one of you contributes towards monthly upkeep then maintain separate lists for the two of you.

As was mentioned earlier, in case you have other irregular sources of money, such as the occasional cash sent to you by a relative, or perhaps an unexpected earning when you suddenly decided to sell some of your old things, you do not need to list them down here since they are not regular sources. You can allocate them to other important matters, as you will learn later on. For now, anything that is "extra" should be set aside. Even if you are just on the Listing Stage right now, the time has come for you to practice being more conscious when the money comes in and how it goes out.

Next, make a list of all your necessary monthly bills and payables. Note that this list will only include necessary bills and payables. So don't include anything that you think is not important. This means that you include only those that you cannot possibly be late for or miss completely, such as the rent, utility bills, food, transportation to work, and payment for other things that cover your basic needs for survival and health. You should also include in this list your payments for any debts, since these are things you need to clean up now in order to have a big enough budget for your basic needs later on. An example of this list would be the following:

Essential Monthly Bills and Payables	
Rent/Mortgage	$100.00
Loans/Personal Debts	$15.00
Credit Card	$70.00
Utilities	$35.00
Healthcare/Medicines	$15.00
Gas/Transportation	$20.00
Food/Groceries	$75.00
Education/Classes	$15.00
Personal Care	$5.00
Gym Membership	$20.00
Total Payables per month	$370.00

When it comes to the amount payables, round off each amount to the next higher value. As for your credit card bill, try covering the minimum amount due for now, if that applies. In a later chapter, you can learn of suggestions to manage your credit cards and other debts better.

Remember to include any ongoing memberships you have that require monthly payment, or that you need to set aside a budget for each month. This includes gym memberships or other club fees— anything that you cannot just cut off for now. In fact, these need to be given top priority as they will have to be paid for without fail.

You will discover that after making both lists, you fall under one of two major categories. You will find out that either you earn more than what you spend or you spend more than what you earn. However, take note that these are just your basic payables for the month. It still does not include leisurely activities and other social obligations. Even if you fall under the first category where you earn more than what you spend, it might still not be reflected in your current financial situation since you may learn later on in the next chapters that a big chunk of your money goes to non-necessities first before the regular monthly necessities. So don't jump to conclusions and assume thongs by looking at your initial two lists. This activity is only meant for you to get started on a good habit. Once you inculcate the habit you will have a chance to be up to date with all your earnings and expenditures. Let us now look at some things that you will have to bear in mind while preparing your lists.

Place
When you decide to prepare a list, remember to assign yourself a particular place where you are most comfortable. You must not have any distractions around you as they can cause you to get disturbed and you might commit an error. Remember that errors can cause you to miscalculate and your budget will be thrown off track. Find yourself a quiet corner and switch off the television or any other forms of media. It is believed that those who prepare their lists in the mornings will have a chance to do it faster and in

an efficient manner as opposed to those that do it at night. Sit on a desk and chair and finish it off at the earliest.

Time

Just like assigning the activity a set place, you need to assign it a set time. This means that you think of a time that is best for you to prepare your list. As was mentioned earlier, you can choose to do it in the morning and dedicate no more than 30 minutes for it. Evenings are also fine as long as you are not drowsy or lazy. When it comes to the day, you can choose either the first day of the month or the last day. It is best that you choose the first day as you would have received your salary and can prepare an inclusive list. The last day might mean not having a chance to include some of the incomes but this day will be good to plan out the expenses for the coming month.

Stationary

Make sure you have everything ready and in place before you start preparing your list. The more organized that you remain, the faster that you will be able to complete your task. So have your journal and pen in place or keep your digital diary ready. You must not get up and roam around until you are done preparing the list and must remain put in one place. In case you do need something then quickly run up to get it and don't waste time in doing so.

Statements

For easy recording of all your incomes, you can make use of statements. Start by gathering all your statement documents and file them neatly. Now look at the name of the document, record it in the description and then record the amount that is pertaining to it. As was mentioned earlier, record even the smallest of detail and round off the amounts that end in loose change. To make it easier for you, you can fill out the descriptions and keep it ready for next time. All you have to do is add in the values and you will be done. The same applies to your spouse's lists. If you are preparing it for them, then ask them to hand over their salary statements, interest statements, any certificate deposits etc. You can then either prepare a separate list for them or add it into one inclusive list.

Receipts/ bills
Just like the income statements, you need to record all the bills and receipt values in your expenses column. For this, you can gather all your bills and receipts and stack their hard copies to use as reference. Make sure you collect them and have them ready to be used before you sit down to prepare the list as running around to get them at the last minute will waste your time and distract you. Again, you can prepare the columns and fill in the usual types of bill names and simply type in or write down the numbers each time.

Calculator
It is vital that you add up the numbers accurately and arrive at the correct sum. You cannot put in wrong amounts and if there are a lot of numbers to add up then you should use a calculator. You can also make use of an app that will take all your numbers and show the final total at the bottom or just an excel sheet will do. Just be sure to make an accurate recording of the amount.

Update
You need to update your lists every 15 days. Many people do not do this and think that they are on schedule. But you will have to update your list from time to time and add or subtract things from it. Say for example you had an unexpected expense. You must record it in your list and write the amount in the expenses column and call it "unexpected expenses". Similarly, you need to update

the list from time to time and make sure that you are up to date with it.

Reminder

It is easy to forget about the list and this can especially happening during the initial stages. To help you remember to prepare a list, you can make use of an alarm to remind you. Some people associate making the list to a routine that they follow and try and finish the list within 30 minutes before the routine. Say for example you watch a show at 7 pm. You should prepare the list at 6.30 and be done with it to sit and leisurely watch your show. This will help you remember better and allow you to turn the activity into a routine habit.

These are just the essential steps that you need to follow while you prepare your list and if there are any additional things that you wish to do then you can incorporate them in your list making schedule.

Chapter 3

Balance

In this chapter, you will make use of the two lists that you made in the previous chapter. This time, you will evaluate your listed payables to see if any adjustment can be made as early as now by looking at alternative options for those items. Again, these are suggested measures, and they are applied particularly to the examples used in this book. Feel free to apply it to your version of payables as necessary.

Based on the sample lists in the previous chapter, you see that the payables have a higher total than the income:

Total Income: $355.00

Total Payable: $370.00

Take note that even if the total payable amount is smaller than the total income, its evaluation is still essential. Right now, even at this early step, you are trying to free up some money which can go to many things that could be more important or beneficial in the long run. It is perfectly understandable that everything you currently spend for now, whether they are monthly payables or not, all seem like a necessity. However, this evaluation shall put all these things into perspective so that it will be much clearer and easier for you to recognize that while all may seem important, each payable or expense still has its own level of importance. Some will need to go before the others while the rest will just need to wait a bit.

So, given your list of payables, you can now try to evaluate if something is absolutely necessary or if it is something you can do without or put off for now. Remember, even if you take off something from your list now, it may only be just a temporary arrangement, as you are evaluating each item according to its importance or necessity. In some cases, you can even take off an item in order to replace it with something that either costs less or nothing. Whatever your thoughts or reasons are for keeping or scrapping each item, write them down next to the list so you can go back to it later on. It also helps to write down notes for better processing. Based on the given example:

Essential Monthly Bills and Payables		Notes
Rent/Mortgage	$100.00	Absolutely essential; no other place to stay in now
Loans/Personal Debts	$15.00	Absolutely essential; need to keep this going for good record
Credit Card	$70.00	Absolutely essential; need to keep this going for good record
Utilities	$35.00	Only the water, electricity, internet connection, and phone line are crucial now. Perhaps I can have the cable connection cut off for now since I very rarely watch TV anymore. Cost will go down to $30.

Essential Monthly Bills and Payables		Notes
Healthcare/Medicines	$15.00	I can just buy smaller doses of vitamins instead of the bigger bottles since I often forget to take them every day. I can do with fewer supplies each month. Cost will go down to $10.
Gas/Transportation	$20.00	I can avoid bringing the car or taking a cab, and just stick to other public transportation options. Cost will go down to $10.
Food/Groceries	$75.00	I can just buy the exact amount of food I actually consume each month, with just a little extra. This shall also prevent me from having too many leftovers that I throw away eventually. Cost will go down to $60.

Essential Monthly Bills and Payables		Notes
Education/Classes	$15.00	I miss most of my language/pottery/ dressmaking class anyway so it is either I regularly attend it to get my money's worth or I stop going altogether and save the money. Since I really want to learn it, I shall continue paying, except this time, I shall really commit to attending.
Personal Care	$5.00	Absolutely essential.
Gym Membership	$20.00	I can opt to run early in the morning or after work. Or follow those free workout routines online. Cost will go down to zero.
Total Payables per month	$370.00	Total Payables down to $215. I have cut down my payables by $155.

In case you are wondering why the list of income is not being evaluated, it is not that there is no need to do so. In fact, you can also look at it to review other better options for earning more. It will allow you to save more money on a monthly basis. Say for example you are getting 100$ through interest or rent, you can decide to try and maximize that amount by investing more money in the same avenue and be left with a lot more money at the end of the month. However, it is better to begin working with what you currently have, and what you currently have are your current sources of income and the things that you absolutely need to spend for in order to survive and stay healthy. Hence, you are evaluating the payables first.

Going back to the above list with its evaluation notes, you can see in the example that some payables have already been identified as less essential. They may still be important, but at this stage of working on being debt-free, they can be replaced by other things that cost less, hence freeing up some money that can be allocated to other things. Remember that this is only temporary and you are doing it to try and repay your debt as soon as possible and improve your life at the earliest. You can always return to these unimportant expenses once you are debt free. Until then, you may have to compromise a little. In the evaluation only a few of the hobby classes were cut down upon. You can still continue with any one of your classes as it will help you remain distracted.

However, in case you feel a bit of regret or sadness for having to let go of some activities or things, take a look at the amount of money that you could be saving for now for each month. In the above example, there is suddenly an extra amount of money worth $155.00. If your lists and evaluation come up with an extra too, then in the next chapter, you can see how this will immediately be of use, and how this time, you are not limited to spend only on your monthly essentials. Perhaps you can have some budget for a few leisurely things or activities that will still put some balance into your life, and you are not merely tied to your financial obligations.

Remember that the evaluations provided here are just imaginary and meant to give you a head start. You need to come up with your own form of reasoning. It will not be the same for everyone and you cannot extrapolate the same measures to all your lists. Your priorities will change every month and you need to prepare a different budget list for the month. If you wish to stick to the same list then it will not be ideal. Once you understand how your life is still pretty much the same despite cutting down on 155$ worth of activities, you will develop the confidence to make that number bigger. You might start cutting down on more of these unnecessary expenses and have enough to pay off your debts on time. So, it is important to evaluate your lists from time to time and remain as up to date with it as possible.

On the other hand, if you were only able to trim down your payables to simply match the income, then that is still good. In the next chapters, you can learn of ideas on how to either increase your source of income, or lessen your payables, or even both.

In the event that your payables are still greater than your income, perhaps another evaluation is essential until you are able to at least match them. Then, move on to the next chapters. Spend some time and look at each of the expenses in detail. Sometimes, it is easy to get confused and not have a clear understanding of the expenses. It might seem a little blurry as it will be your first time trying to cut down on your routine expenses. But you must remain persistent and try and match or reduce your expenses. If you need help, then ask a smart friend or a sibling to help you out with your list. They might suggest cutting down on something that will allow you to reduce your expenses. It always pays to have the opinion of another person as they will have an outsiders view and tell you where you need to make amendments. In all this, keep in mind your vision of yourself being debt-free and having financial freedom. Once you have that as an inspiration, you will automatically make all the right moves. If you feel sad at the prospect of not attending a hobby class then think of how many you can actually join once you have repaid all your debt and are completely debt free.

Chapter 4

Chart

By now, you should have at least matched your income with your most basic payables. You can then make a chart or a table joining your two lists. We looked at how through evaluation you can successfully cut down on 155$ a month. Again, that was for the example that we are using in this book and yours might be different from ours.

Monthly Income		Monthly Payables	
Company Pay	$155.00	Rent/Mortgage	$100.00
Part-time Job	$135.00	Loans/Personal Debts	$15.00
Sales from homemade cookies	$45.00	Credit Card	$70.00
Paid errands	$20.00	Utilities	$30.00
		Healthcare/ Medicines	$10.00
		Gas/ Transportation	$10.00
		Food/Groceries	$60.00
		Education/ Classes	$15.00
		Personal Care	$5.00
Total Income	355.00	Total Payable	$215.00

As computed earlier, the adjustments in payables amounted to an extra cash of $155.00. You can now allocate this to other expenses. In order to decide which to spend this extra cash on, look at all your other regular expenses in a month that did not fall under the category of necessities and make a list of them. For example:

- Night out with old friends
- Coffee or drinks with another set of friends
- Sports activities
- Supplies for a creative hobby
- Shopping for apparel
- Shopping for household items and other household needs
- Savings for emergencies
- Travel fund

Depending on how much you are able to save, you can select at least one item from the list above and then allocate your extra fund accordingly. Choose the one that you find most important for you. If you cannot choose which ones to prioritize since they may be equally important at various occasions, you can do this another way.

Income		Main Payables		Other Expenses
Company Pay	$155.00	Rent/ Mortgage	$100.00	Night out with friends
Part-time Job	$135.00	Loans/ Personal Debts	$15.00	Coffee or drinks
Sales from homemade cookies	$45.00	Credit Card	$70.00	Sports
Paid errands	$20.00	Utilities	$30.00	Supplies for hobby

Income		Main Payables		Other Expenses
		Healthcare/ Medicines	$10.00	Shopping for apparel
		Gas/Trans-portation	$10.00	Shopping for household
		Food/ Groceries	$60.00	Emergency fund
		Education/ Classes	$15.00	Travel fund
		Personal Care	$5.00	

You can create a chart which has the latest table of both your income and payables, and then include all these other items that you usually spend on too. As the extra money comes in, you can allocate accordingly. You can also choose to have these other expenses "take turns." This way, you have your urgent bills and payables covered, and you still have some to spend for other leisurely activities or other items that you wish to buy.

Remember that these expenses are imaginary and something we came up with. You can modify your expenses as per your needs. You can adjust the amount that you contribute towards your night out with friends with that of your travel fund and vice versa. As long as you are able to fulfill all your basic needs you will have it easy for you. Remember that saving for debt does not mean stopping living altogether. It just means that you remain careful with how you spend your existing money and how much you can save to pay off your debts.

The idea is also that each month, you have a record of all the cash flow so that you can be sure your money goes to the right payables first, and then to the other items in your list after the urgent payables have been covered. In the event that you decide to add other expenses, you can easily refer to your list and see how each compares against the others. If not, you can quickly go back to your records of your previous months to see which of these other expenses you often end up spending on.

This method may feel very rigid at first, and as the months go by you may feel like you are depriving yourself or that there suddenly seems so little to go around. However, when it starts to feel this way or when you are feeling like you are scrimping so much on yourself, remember these three things:

1. You are doing this for the sake of your vision of being debt-free and having financial freedom. This will just be temporary, at the least, until your new finances stabilize and improve. So don't go too hard on yourself and regret anything. Everything in life is a learning curve and something that will help you lead a better life. You cannot hope to have everything consistently available all through your life. There will be down phases and also up phases. They alternate and if you are having a down phase now then you are sure to have an up phase soon enough.

2. Though you may feel like you cannot splurge as much as you did before, remember that you are at least sure that all your important payables are covered. It would be much worse and troublesome if you had spent for new things but have your urgent bills pending and unpaid. Regardless of how much or how little you can spend for luxury or leisure, you can be guilt-free when it comes to your main financial responsibilities. Also, when you continue this practice, remember that your credit card bills and other debts are being paid off in increments, and doing so continuously will eventually finish them up and you will have a chance to live freely. There is no point in remaining tied down by expenses that are worthless. This includes all

those expenses you incur on a monthly basis through your credit card bills. Remain as happy as possible since you will soon be debt free and capable of living a much better life, after paying off debts, than you have been thus far.

3. Because of your evaluation of your monthly payables, you may have been able to set aside some extra cash that can go to other expenses that have more to do with your personal leisurely activities than your main financial obligations. Even though this may be just a small amount for now, recognize that this still balances your finances in that you get to experience the fruits of your labor not only through the coverage of your monthly bills, but also through the other simple joys you can experience every now and then, such as the occasional night out with friends, or shopping for those art supplies, or perhaps the new cleaning products for the house that you wish to try out. So these will keep you going until you are completely done with your debt and in a position to lead a normal life again. Remember that you can always have the life you dreamt of by paying off all your debts and the kind of happiness that you and your family face will help you remain stress free.

Eventually, these benefits will evolve into greater measures. Remember that it is usually the initial adjustments that seem the most difficult, especially as you go deeper into the practice and start to feel the changes they have made in your life. Think long-term as this is what you are working on for now. Again, remember your vision of being debt free and having financial freedom. Remain strong through this phase in order to pay off all your debt on time. If you delay paying up then you will only suffer more. You need to think of your debts as things that are not worth paying extra for and the sooner that you deal with it, the faster that your life improves. So regardless of whether you have a small debt or a large one, you should make all possible efforts to pay it off at the earliest and live a life of freedom.

Chapter 5

Adjust

You now have a basic chart that you can use and update for each month whenever money comes in and goes out. Just label each according to the month you are keeping a record of. Hence, whenever a set of income is received, you can immediately and clearly allocate it to the corresponding bill or payable, thus completing your urgent expenses first. Anything in excess can then be spent on or saved for an item in your Other Expenses column as you wish.

Just for the sake of a quick rundown of what you have accomplished so far:

- You made a list of your regular income and your regular bills and payables.

- You have balanced these lists through the evaluation of your payables in order to make them smaller in amount than your income, or, you have at least matched them so that all the basic payables are covered.

- You have created a chart where you can record your money flow, while having a list of other expenses to which you can allocate any extra money.

This chart is now your main tool for now in tracking your expenses and reviewing your money flow. It will be your main record for each month, so just be mindful of filing them accordingly for easy and quick access and reference later on. With just one look, you can see how much money has come in, where it went, and which items are still not covered. Basically, all it has now are details on the money you currently possess, and the payables where you intend to allocate the money. Now, we look at how to improve the contents of this chart, particularly in terms of the money coming in.

Of course, a lifestyle change should be in place, but you shall learn more about that in the next chapter. That involves a longer time frame and more consistent practice. The methods you are about to learn from this chapter are quicker and more instantaneous in terms of effect, so it would be better to take a look at these first. Basically, these are ways for you to earn some quick cash, which can help with your other payables and savings.

These ways of earning may not bring a fixed or regular income each month, but they are still additional sources of money. If you wish, you can even dedicate one method completely for one payable; for example, every time you hold a yard sale, you are dedicated to putting all those earnings to a debt payment, or to add to a credit card payment. It is really up to you where you allocate these extra earnings, but it would surely help if you tried these out on particular schedules throughout the year:

A Yard Sale

You can do this once or twice a year. Hold a big, nice one, and really go all-out on clearing clutter from your home. This is a good way to do three things in one go: you clean up your space, you let go of things you do not use but may be useful to others, and you earn from it.

To do this effectively, you have to keep in mind that it is good to let go of all those things that no longer serve you. Remember, a clearer space also contributes to a clearer mind, so you really clean up your space on various levels. Best of all, you convert all these unused things into cash.

Before you put the goods on sale try and restore them and find their original boxes and price tags. People love having things that are restored and you will be able to sell better. You can choose to scratch the price and put in your reduced price and it is sure to bring in some money. Remember that absolutely anything goes in a yard sale and you need not ponder over whether or not an item is suitable. You can add any item to your sale be it your children's toys, games, old clothes, old jewelry, shoes, electronics, kitchenware, accessories etc.

If you are still left with a few items and do not wish to take it back home then you can decide to either donate it or sell it in a secondary market. Remember that the more you give, the more you receive. So if you are to give things away to a charity then you will get back double in return. It will make you happy and remain satisfied for a long time. If you have things that are new and unused then listing them on eBay or Amazon will help you sell them easily. All you have to do is take pictures of them and upload them with a short description. They will fly off of your shelf faster than you can blink. But if even that fails then you can ask if any of your friends or relatives need it and try and make a little cash out of them instead of throwing them away.

Earning From Your Hobby

Think of ways on how you can earn from your hobby. This way, you will be earning from doing something you love. For instance, if you like to paint, make small paintings that you can sell. If you like to cook, sell packed food or desserts. If you like to dance, you can give informal dancing lessons. If you like sewing or crocheting, sell some of your handmade items. There is also the idea of gardening and selling your produce to the local market. If you have a large collection of books then consider opening a library. It is easy to make use of whatever that you have and employ it to earn you a few extra dollars a month. Your investment will be zero but your returns might run into the hundreds. But remember to do it with full heart as half hearted measures do not bear fruits.

The schedule for this method of earning is up to you. You can sell items from your house and just have a page online for your merchandise, or you can start selling off your creations to your friends who will then recommend your product or service to others. Try and build up your network as much as possible. You will be able to sell your stuff to more and more people. Don't limit yourself to just your acquaintances and try and find other people who will encourage your work and allow you to expand.

When you create, you can do so in your free time, and since it is your hobby, it will not feel so much like work to you as long as you keep it manageable too. Then, set a schedule on when you intend to welcome visitors who will look at your merchandise, when you can make deliveries if applicable, or when you can hold lessons you want to teach.

You can even join clubs or occasionally participate in market fairs where you can find opportunities to sell and market yourself.

There are hundreds of ways in which you can make the most of your hobby. There are people out there who despite having no talent will engage in activities that will help them earn money. So if you have something that you think will allow you to not just showcase your talent but also make the most of it, then don't waste any more time and start using it to your advantage.

Taking on another Sideline
While you may have a part-time job or two, perhaps taking on a less tedious and less time-consuming job is something you can

consider. For example, there are online jobs where you can write articles for others, and you can do the writing in your free time, wherever you are, given its online nature. You can also take on language tutorials, if you are particularly proficient in any language. If the previous method utilizes your hobbies, this time, you can also use your other skills that others require. As mentioned, you can use your writing skills or your knowledge of other languages. If you can cook well, you can even offer to be the paid cook for a neighbor or acquaintance for a party. Think of what you can do and you will surprise yourself with how many ways there are for you to earn extra money. If you have two hobbies that you are good at then there is nothing better than to pursue both. You can make use of your writing and cooking skills and come up with a writing blog that is aimed at amateurs or cooks. If you are good at physical training then train a few clients and make money out of it. You can also start yoga classes and get people to join in. it is best to do things at your own place as you can avoid commuting and paying rents for services used.

You will also have the chance to be more relaxed and in a position to do your work leisurely. There are a million things that you can do to make a few extra dollars and it only requires you to put in a little effort. You don't have to go out of your way to learn new things and apply them as you will already be well versed in the things required to carry out these jobs. You can start and stop at will and have a good time while employing your talents.

Don't think of these as being tedious or time consuming, they are called part time for a reason. You can start with your side job at the earliest and start making the most of your spare time. After you pay off all your debt you can stop pursuing your side job. There will be no obligation but if you are comfortable with it then you can continue with it to have a parallel income and a chance to save money on a monthly basis.

Your earnings from these methods can significantly help you cover various expenses. Moreover, you do not need to do them all the time, so it is not as tedious and time-consuming as your regular, daily jobs. You can even find other ideas and opportunities as you do them.

When you earn any additional income, this will have a good reflection on the finance chart you have created. You will have your payables covered, and you may even have enough budget for the other things you want to allocate the money to. What's more, you might even see occasions when the income spills over to the budget of the following month. It may not happen all the time, but it is possible when you really become able to see the opportunities for you to have additional sources of income.

In chapter 2, you evaluated your payables in terms of their importance and urgency. Now that you are looking at ways to beef up your income, there is also another good suggestion for you to possibly lessen your payable, or, at least, make it more manageable. This has to do with your bank loans or credit card bills. It may or may not apply to you, depending on your arrangements with your bank, but it is worth a try.

Talk to your bank or debtor, and see if you can ask for a fixed amount to be paid each month, which will no longer require you to pay any additional interest charges. This time, since you can manage your budget better than before and you can allocate a fixed amount to your payables given your income, then perhaps you can come up with a good arrangement with your bank or debtor. What's important here, though, is that you really need to pay the amount you agreed to pay for each month. You may feel tied down to a fixed expense each month, but this also means you just made the end of the payment period much easier to see. It also becomes less threatening because you are no longer worried about the growing interest charges.

Do your best to make these adjustments—your new methods to earn additional income and your possibly better arrangements with the bank—and these can certainly have positive long-term effects on your finances. You have just moved closer to enjoying financial freedom and finishing off your debts. Sure, it may take some time, but you are still moving forward, and you are no longer stuck.

Chapter 6

Change

By this time, you may be looking back and seeing how many adjustments you have made, and you even feel how much things have changed, especially in terms of your spending habits. Perhaps now, you find yourself not being able to spend so much anymore, but surely you feel great about being able to cover your basic and urgent payables. Sometimes it does feel like you are in a pinch all the time, but as you follow through and commit to better finance practices, things will definitely get better. To fast track this improvement, your new financial habits will also require a lifestyle change.

You may probably be feeling already that a lifestyle change has taken place ever since you committed to prioritizing your urgent bills and payables. However, there is one basic rule on how to make a truly effective lifestyle change:

Live within your means.

This means you only spend within the budget that you have. You do not spend borrowed money for leisure or luxury or anything you do not need, even more so when you already have a budget for all the basic needs. You do not lead a lifestyle that you cannot afford.

Many people have the habit of borrowing money and deciding to use it for a luxury as a treat for the sacrifices that they have made. But imagine how much faster you will be able to pay off your debt if you save this money and contribute it towards debt repayment.

Naturally, it will be tough at first, but keep in mind your vision that this is all for a financially free, debt-free you. You cannot use any money for useless purposes as you will definitely regret it later. You will feel bad for having spent money on something that gave you only temporary happiness and there was nothing sustainable in it.

You must try and make all the best decisions for yourself and not give into temptations. Imagine what would happen if were to spend up all your money now and have lots of debt in your old age. Is that not a very scary prospect? Remember too that you will eventually get used to the new lifestyle you are living. It does not mean that you will get used to a life where you scrimp all the time or have to think about budgets all the time. In fact, it is quite the contrary.

When you have learned to manage your finances more effectively and when you have paid off all your debts, you will then feel a level of financial freedom that is not all about having lots of money, but being able to manage it well while living very comfortably. But for this phase to come through, you need to learn the things that will help you remain money savvy. For some it can be an in born trait while others might have to learn it. Don't worry if you are incapable of learning something new fast enough. You will eventually get there and once you do, you will be able to live an amazing life. And then, you will not be thinking about whether your budget can handle something; you will instead be thinking more about whether something is worth it, or if you even need it. You will no longer have the compulsion to just spend.

Your mindset will have changed from simply counting the money to discerning whether the money you already freely have is worth spending for something. You will have become wiser about money, and you will be very content with how you have managed the journey well from the time you started making your lists to the time you have managed to stick to your financial commitments, until such time that you are simply benefitting from all your efforts and decisions. So try and live within your means now, in order to lead a merrier life later. Don't be bothered by small things and try and remain as happy and content as possible. Once all your debt is paid for, you will have the best life and can also start living luxuriously.

Chapter 7

Moving Forward

Paying off all your debts and balancing out your finances may not happen overnight, but you will begin to experience the benefits of doing something about them as you go along. Now, as you move forward, here are some guidelines that you can follow in order to keep yourself on track as you utilize your finance chart and do the methods for you to earn extra.

Continue to live within your means.

As taught in the previous chapter, you live within the lifestyle you can afford. You can upgrade when your finances do. Meanwhile, especially during the time you are starting to make adjustments, you will need to function within the means available to you. As you move forward, stick to this principle so that you no longer experience budget troubles or finances getting out of hand. Again, you will have to remain strong and willful. You cannot give into temptations and must remain within your budget. There can be several distractions but you need to remain as away from them as possible. You need to remind yourself every now and then that you are leading a life of compromise only to lead a better life later. Your confines are temporary and something that you will be done with in no time. You can prepare a chart that will show where you stand now and where you can be in a few years' time. Looking at the chart will help you remain in your confines. It will allow you to do things that are important for you and also help you earn extra money that can be contributed towards your savings.

Spend using cash as much as possible.

It is good to have a credit or debit card on hand for online or specific purchases, but be sure to pay them with the cash available to you right away. Otherwise, try to stick to cash when spending. This will reinforce your practice of living within your means. You must make it a point to carry only cash when you go out to purchase something big. Have two wallets with you. Fill up one with money and the other one with just cards. Depending on the kind of trip that you wish to take, carry the wallet that is befitting. Do not take just cards with you even if it is to do with a card requisite trip. Try and use cash as much as possible. When it comes to online payments, you can use your online banking method and draw from your account. Don't be tempted to use the credit cards. You need to curb using your cards as much as possible when you have to take care of debts. You can choose to take a friend along when you go shopping. They will keep an eye on you and prevent you from using cards. They will encourage you to take your cash out and you will be satisfied with your trip. Remember to always carry a journal or a diary and write down how much cash you spent. You can keep track of it with ease. It will help you know exactly how much was used and how much you are left with.

Schedule big purchases and trips

Since trips and big items cost a lot, schedule them. Save up. Include a travel fund in your Other Expenses column if you must. Never just go on a trip or make a big purchase on a whim. You are now spending wisely, and spending money for something else or money you do not have yet is not helpful to what you are trying to achieve. Later on, when you have saved enough money for travels or expensive items, then you can do so, but until then, persevere to save and wait until you have enough. Again, this is just for now, as you strive towards better financial conditions. This is not permanent. You might also have problems initially but you will soon learn to schedule your trips and be in a position to plan in advance. You need not spend thinking about whether or not your trip is worth it. Most people plan purchasing trips at the beginning of the month and buy everything that they will need for the rest of it. This will help you remain within budget and you will not feel stressed about your shopping trips.

Stick to your budget

To sum it all up, stick to your budget. When you do, you become able to live within your means. You spend only the cash that you have. You do not get ahead and spend what is yet to come. Stick to your budget, and soon enough, this budget will grow, all because you seriously committed to making a change in your financial life. You can have reminders placed all over your house just so that you don't surpass your budget. You need to have reminders on your laptop as well so that you don't buy things impulsively over the net. Try and remain as strict with your spending as possible. One way to remain within budget is to reward yourself from time to time. Remain within your budget and also try and save some money from it. Whatever that you are left with can be used to treat yourself. You can go to a spa or take a weekend off. You can also buy yourself a nice meal or some chocolates and ice creams! It will motivate you to remain within your budget and you will have enough to pay off all your debts in no time.

As you follow what you have learned from the previous chapters and stick to these guidelines, you will just naturally find yourself getting out of debt more smoothly. Eventually, you will just have paid off all your debts, and the money that used to go to their payments can be allocated to other things. All that effort to gain financial freedom will have worked for you. You will be in a very good position to lead a life that is free from worry and also have the option of spending as much as you like. You will free your family from the problems that come with having lots of debts. Ultimately, you will lead a nice and happy life. Acknowledge the fact that you have taken the necessary measures to improve your financial status and soon enough, you will finally, truly be free.

Chapter 8

401(k) Contributions While In Debt

A lot of people in debt become unsure or wonder if they should continue to contribute to their 401(k) plan as it will slow down paying off their debt. Should you forgo contributing to your 401k plan? The answers is no. You will learn four reasons not to stop contributing to your retirement plan. I understand that being in debt is uncomfortable for most people. While you are paying off your debt, you need to build your retirement savings. By contributing to your 401(k) plan you can reap the benefits of the tax advantages of a retirement savings account make it financially favorable for you to contribute and invest through them.

4 Reasons to Not Touch Your 401(k)

1. An employer match on a 401(k) is a good thing and you should take advantage of it.
   - It is wise to take advantage of contributing to a 401(k), up to the point where the employer matches your contributions.
   - They are essentially just giving you extra money.
   - Contribute up to the full match and use the rest to pay off your debt.

2. The money you contribute to your 401(k) has decades to grow.

   - The sooner you start putting money into the plan, the longer it has to grow and accumulate more money for you.
   - When you factor in the employer's match, you're doing a lot better than not having anything at all.

3. Every time you get a raise in the future add half of percentage of the raise to your 401k.

- By taking a small percentage of your salary increase, that amount should go to your 401K plan to continue to build up your retirement account.
- Use the remaining percentage of your salary increase not contributed to help pay your debt.

4. Borrow against 401(k).

- If you are going to withdrawal from your 401(k), make sure it is a loan against the account.
- By borrowing from your 401(k) plan, you continue to contribute into the account, but the majority of the contribution goes to pay back the loan, until it's paid back in full.
- You will lose a little by borrowing from the 401(k) therefore you should check with your plan's provider for details about borrowing against your money.
- The real big drawback to borrowing against your 401(k) is, if you should leave your job for any reason such as being laid off or being fired, you will have to immediately come up with the balance that you owe.

The only time I would say not to contribute would be if you have had several emergencies come up in your life, which you will need to build up your emergency fund quickly. If you need to stop contributing to your 401(k) plan try to keep it to one month or two months at most without adding to it. This way you will be able to get back and continue building your path to your financial freedom quickly.

Now that you know why you should not dip into your 401(k) plan unless it's of an extreme emergency. Let's go learn and apply the most practical method for reducing your consumer debt as quickly as possible for you can get out of debt and start heading towards your financial freedom.

Chapter 9

5 Steps To Reduce Consumer Debt For Your Financial Freedom

The 5 Steps you are about to learn is perhaps the most effective credit card and consumer debt payment process there is. It is a simple process and like all things that are truly simple, it is amazingly effective that it will amaze you. This will give you a clear map to follow that will enable you to get debt free. You will be amazed on how quickly it will take you to become debt-free.

Step 1. Discipline Yourself to use only 1 or 2 Credit Cards

- The first step in starting this process is to develop the habit that you will not add any additional long-term debt. It is does not get any simpler than that.
- You MUST discipline yourself to only use ONLY 1 or 2 credit cards for any additional charges you must make. If you are going to use a card to make any charges, you should, use the card that has the lowest balance.
- Any new charges that you add to your credit cards, you must pay them off full every month. You must commit to reduce or break the habit of incurring more debt.

Step 2. Come Up With an extra $150-$200 per month

- This second step is very important step of the process. You must be able to come up with an extra $150-$200 per month. This amount will be your launch pad to becoming debt-free from your consumer debt.
- You need to know that if you cannot come up with an extra $150-$200 a month, your chances of becoming debt-free and having financial freedom will probably never happen.

Step 3. Apply the $150-$200 To ONLY one of Your Credit Cards

- The third step you are going to do is that you are going to pay the minimum amount due for the month PLUS the $150-$200 you came up with towards one of your credit card(s).
- For any other credit cards that you have, you will just pay the minimum amount due for the month on those other cards.
- The mistake that most people make that I know of and I did was to pay a little extra each month on all your cards. It was no surprise that the cards were never getting paid off and seeing the interests charge increase next month's balance.

Step 4. Apply Amount You Were Paying To Your Next Credit Card

- The fourth step of the process is once you have completely paid off your first credit card, you will apply the total amount (Minimum Amount + $150-$200) that your were paying on that card each month towards your next credit card.

- You are now going to pay the minimum amount due on the second card plus the total monthly payments that you were paying on your first credit card (Minimum Amount + $150-$200).
- You continue doing this process with any other credit cards and any other consumer credit debt that you have. You will see how fast you be paying off those credit cards.

Step 5. Pay Off Any Remaining Debts

- The fifth step is that once you have paid off all your credit cards and any other consumer debt that you had, you can continue to use what was taught in Steps 3 and Steps 4 to pay off things such as you car loans and house payments.

By committing to the 5 Steps described above, you must have complete faith that your goal of becoming debt-free and beginning your road towards financial freedom is achievable. Remember that if you believe in it, then it will surely happen. Once you have paid off your last debt and are now completely debt-free, you can take those monthly payments that you were making and put that amount towards investments. You can start building an asset column and generating additional income for yourself. I need you to now take action and commit to following this simple process of paying off your debt.

Chapter 10

Steps To Repay Debt

When it comes to repaying the debt, you need to make use of certain steps that will help you repay it in an organized manner. Imagine having to do something without knowing what the next step should be, it will only cause you to lose interest in the process. So it is important for you to follow a set method so that you can repay your loans as soon as possible and return back to a normal life. Let us now look at these steps in detail.

Start with a plan

The first step involves starting out with a plan. This means that you sit down and decide on how you wish to repay your debts. You can sit with a journal and pen and write down the type of method that will suit you. There are two types of methods that you can adopt to repay your debts viz. the snowballing method and the avalanche method. These two methods are discussed in detail a little later in this chapter. Once you make up on the type of method, you can proceed to the next step of this process.

Arrange

Start by arranging your debts in an order that makes it easier for you to start repaying. Most people prefer to list the highest debt amount first as that will invite the highest rate of interest. It is important to taper towards the lowest amount as these might not be a major cause of concern. But it is also okay to start with the lowest amount and move to the highest. It will depend on whatever suits your repaying capacity. Remember to make three columns and write the creditor's name in the first, the amount borrowed in the second and the rate of interest in the third. You should have a clear idea of how much has been borrowed from whom.

Budget

The next step is to prepare a budget for yourself. It is extremely important to prepare a budget as you will know how much needs to be spent on repaying debts. You would have already prepared your income and expenses lists and once you know how much money is left with you, you can split it between debt repayment and savings. Remember that your debt repayment amount should be higher than your savings amount. But don't use all of it to just repay your debts and force yourself to contribute towards your savings.

Intimate

Before you start to repay your debts, you can intimate your creditor. You can call them up and tell them that you are ready to repay your debts. Sometimes, it is good to build a rapport with the creditor. It gives you a chance to speak to them and convey your interest in repaying your debt at the earliest. You need not go over the top in telling them about your plans and just tell them that you are now ready to pay them and that you will be able to repay it within a short time.

Negotiate

When you communicate with your creditor, try and negotiate with them. This generally does not work but if you have been regularly paying the interest and are in a position to repay within a couple of months ten you can ask for a small discount. Remember that this might not always work but you can try your luck. You can at least call them up and ask them to lower the rate of interest for the last 2 or 3 installments so that you save some money. Remember to be prepared for anything and don't get too disappointed if they refuse to listen to your request.

These steps will help you repay your debt in an organized way. Let us now look at the two ways in which you can repay your debts.

Types of repayment

Snowballing

The snowballing method is one of the ways in which you can repay your debt. In this type, you start by repaying the loan amount that is the lowest and slowly move towards the higher values. Just like how a snowball starts small but starts gathering more snow and becomes big. For this, you will have to list your debt amount in such a way that the lowest one is mentioned first and the highest one is mentioned last. You start by repaying the lowest and not move to the next until it is fully paid for.

The biggest advantage of this method is the psychological effect that it has on the person. When the person starts to repay his or her loan and is able to finish paying off at least one of them, then he or she feels confident of paying the rest and works hard towards making it possible. This method is also preferred owing to how easy it is to follow. As soon as the person comes into money, he or she can start repaying. Its simplicity makes it a preferred method as there is no need to calculate any interest rates or come up with a detailed action plan. It is possible to start repaying at the earliest without wasting too much time.

The main disadvantage of this method is that, the higher values will always invite a higher rate of interest. This will cause the final amount to shoot up and the person will have to pay more than what was required of him or her to pay. The small ones will always have a low interest rate and can be paid off easily but keeping the big ones till the end will mean having to pay a large amount of interest along with the principle value.

Avalanche

The avalanche method is the other way in which you can repay your loans. This method is also quite popular and in fact, I much more preferred than the previous method. As per this method, the highest amount of debt is repaid first and the person move to paying the lowest one. For this, it is important to list the highest value first and then move lower. So start by recording the highest loan amount first and continue recording in a descending order. You must repay the highest one fully before moving to the lowest amount.

The advantage of this type is that, you will be done with all the big amounts and not have to worry about having to pay a high rate of interest. In fact, once you finish repaying the large sums, you will instantly feel relieved as a major chunk of your loan will be repaid. This can also have a positive impact on the person's psychology and he or she will know that their money is being used in the most optimum method possible. Another advantage is that, the person will be able to save more money when this method is used as opposed to the snowball method.

The disadvantage of this method is that, the initial sum to repay will be extremely large and might discourage the person from paying off debt. It will take a long time for him or her to come up with such a large sum of money and it will cause them psychological problems. Another disadvantage is its complexity. It will be a complex process to understand how much money needs to be repaid to whom and when. The person might get confused trying to calculate all that debt at once. All this can cause the person to shift to the snowballing method.

Remember that both these techniques have their fair share of advantages and disadvantages and you can choose the type that suits your needs. You cannot run away from both as your debts will have to be paid for and are inescapable activities.

Chapter 11

Faster Ways to Repay Debt

In the previous chapter, we looked at the steps that you need to adopt in order to repay your debt and also saw the methods used to pay them off. In this one, we will shift focus to how you can repay your debts faster and be done with it in a shorter time.

Pool it together

One easy way to repay your debt faster is to unify them. For this, you must borrow a lump sum from another bank which offers a lower rate of interest and repay all your creditors at the earliest. Once you do so, you will only have to repay the bank from where you borrowed money. This will make the process simpler and you will have a chance to pay lesser interest. For this, you will have to prove your credit worthiness and produce a clean credit report. So try and remain as timely as possible when repaying your debts so that you have a good credit score. You can look up a bank yourself or ask someone to suggest a bank that offers a lower rate of interest and produce all your other debt related documents to avail the loan.

Pay more than minimum

One of the oldest tricks in the book that allows you to pay your debt on time or before is to pay more than the minimum amount. This means that you decide and pay more than the standard amount that you are required to pay in a month. For this, you must decide on an amount that is at least 10% more than what you pay regularly. This will ensure that you repay all your debts faster. If you have any spare money coming in then you can use that money as well. As long as you stop paying the minimum and pay out more than what is required of you in a month, you are sure to repay your debt way before its actual repayment date.

Borrow from family

It is always a good idea to borrow money from your family member and get done with your debt repayment. This is best as your family member might not charge you a high rate of interest and you can save on a lot of money in the process. You can take from your father, brother, uncle or just about anyone that is in a good position to lend you the money. Even if it takes a month or two for them to give the money to you, you must remain persistent and borrow the money to help repay your debt at the earliest. Remember to ask for the exact money that you owe to your creditors and not less as it will be easier for you to pay everything to the same person as opposed to several others.

Borrow from insurance

Sometimes, it is easy to borrow from your insurance money and repay your debt. You will have to repay your insurance money but can avail instant relief from a high rate of interest. Make sure you produce all the papers so that you have your loan approved without any problems. But don't forget to repay the amount back as you might invite a fine for delayed payments.

Stop using cards

One of the most important things to do while trying to repay your debt faster is to stop using those dreaded credit cards. They will completely throw your debt repayment plans off track and cause you to pay in excess. It is best that you do away with your credit cards altogether to help remain on track with your debt repayment schemes. We will discuss this topic in detail in the next chapter.

Chapter 12

How To Stop Using Credit Cards

When it comes to repaying your debts, credit cards are your worst enemies. They will only cause you to get into more debt and set up a vicious circle. It is therefore extremely important for you to remain as away from your cards as possible to repay your debts on time. Here are some ways that you can adopt to steer clear of using your credit cards to make your purchases.

Cancel some

The very first thing that you have to do is cancel your cards. Call up your credit card company and have them cancel your cards for you. You might have to settle all their scores before you can do away with your cards. You can get rid of all your cards and promise yourself to not buy any more. This can be hard to do but you need to do it in order to reduce your debt as much as possible and repay your existing ones at the earliest.

Don't cancel oldest

When you decide to cancel your cards, remember to never cancel your oldest ones. They will have a good history and contain information on your credit worthiness. You might need these to use as proof for your worthiness in case you have to avail another loan. Try and surrender the latest cards that you have in your position and those that have hardly been used. You must give away cards that have a high rate of interest and if you have two or more old cards that are inviting high interest then consider keeping only the one that is the oldest and has the best record.

Lock them up

If you do not wish to give away cards then consider locking them away safely and not finding a way to reach them. This will help you reduce their usage and you can reduce your debt to a bare minimum. You can lock them up in a locker so that you don't see them as much. You can also put it away in a drawer and keep the key elsewhere. As long as you don't see them regularly, you will be able to forget about them and not feel the need to use them so very often.

Shred them

It is possible for you to psychologically convince yourself to stop using your cards. For this, you will have to take some extreme measure such as shred it using an office shredder or cut it using scissors. You will be motivated to remain away from your cards and not have the interest to buy any more. Just make sure you shred it such that all your personal information is completely erased or destroyed otherwise it might result in identity theft. You can subject all your cards to this treatment at once or do them one by one to drive the point home.

Two wallets

It is always a good idea to have two wallets. This means that you have two separate wallets for your cards and your money. The one that has your cards should have a little cash as well but the cash wallet should have no cards. You can carry the card wallet only when you have to buy small things and use the card only if the cash does not suffice. The cash wallet needs to be carried when you have to make large purchases as you will not have the option of using the card. You can successfully avoid using your card and inviting a large interest.

Use a chart

You need to prepare a chart for yourself that clearly explains why you should not use a credit card. Sometimes, a visual aid helps more than mere reminders. You need to tell yourself why your credit card is evil and what you can do to stay away from it. You need to put in a few pictures as well as mere words will make it boring. You can take a photo of the poster and have it on all your devices to remind you from time to time to not pull out your card and use cash to make your payments.

1.   Debit card/ bank credit card

One idea is to use your debit card instead of cash as it will help you worry less. Carrying cash around might be risky and so, it is a good choice to carry just your debit card, which is linked to your checking account. You can pull it out and use it to make payments for your purchase. Another idea is for you to make use of bank credit cards. These cards are issued by your bank and they will draw from accounts to which you add your own money. There will not be any interest that will be levied but you will have to repay into your account the money that you took out within a specified period of time.

Remove online information

It is important to remove any credit card information that you might have left behind on a site to help you check out easily. The website will maintain this information and use it to pay for your purchases. You might not realize how much you are buying and end up spending a lot of money. So remove all the information from each and every website that you use to make purchases in order to steer clear of your cards being used automatically. You can choose to link it to a debit card or choose online banking as an option to pay for what you buy.

Reward yourself

Once you are completely over with using your credit cards and have just one left with you which you plan to use occasionally, you can reward yourself with something nice. You can choose to take a vacation or take some time off with family and visit a massage center. You can also throw a small party and declare how you are now free from your credit card usage.

Chapter 13

Best Ways To Save Money

By now, you have understood how you can get organized and repay all your debt at the earliest. Next, we will look at what you can do to save money on a monthly basis so that you can direct a substantial amount towards repaying your loans.

These are easy things that you can do on a daily basis and save up to 200$ a month given you follow them religiously.

Get gas cards

One expense that pulls most people down is gas expenses. Paying for gas every week can cost quite a bomb and it is important to save on that money as much as possible. For this, it is best to buy gas cards and add in money on a monthly basis. You might also receive a discount for using this system and save on money. When you have some money that is prepaid, you will make it a point to remain within budget. You will not lose track of how much money you have used up to get your gas and will be in a better position to save on a monthly basis. But remember to not add in too much money at once and have just a little.

Car pool

You must try and car pool as much as possible. It is important for you to save on money on a weekly basis and by car pooling; you will save on both gas and transportation expenses. This is especially important if you have to travel long distances. If you don't have a colleague staying nearby then you can consider asking someone else that you know. You can ask a neighbor to drop you if he or she goes in the same direction as you and try and cut your travel expenses by half per month.

Good car

If you are unable to car pool as often then you can consider buying a fuel efficient car. You can also consider shifting to an electric car and use the charging stations provided by your office to charge your car. The initial cost of the car might be high but you will have a chance to save at least a few hundred dollars by doing so. It is also a good idea to consider buying a second hand car as you are looking to save your money. Don't be shy to buy one and look up for the best possible offer and buy a nice energy efficient car that will help you save money and allow you to repay your debt at the earliest.

Home theater

Many people spend a bomb on their entertainment needs. They will splurge on movie tickets and might also have to pay for friends and family. This can set you back by a few hundred dollars a month. Instead, try and invest in a good home theater system that will give you a similar experience. You can buy a large screen TV and a DVD player and you are all set. You can download torrents from the internet and watch a movie for half the cost. It is fine to buy a second hand television as long as it is in good condition. You can invite friends over to watch and you need not pay for their entertainment.

Coupons

It is always wise to make use of coupons. Coupons are used to pay for groceries that are bought from stores or any other house hold items. It is possible for you to bring down your total payable amount to mere cents just by making use of several coupons. For this, you need to look for a departmental store that accepts coupons in bulk. You will have to collect as many coupons for the month as possible and carry them on your next planned trip. You need to plan in advance and make sure you carry very little cash with you to pay for your items.

Online shopping

It is always wise to shop online for clothes and accessories. You can avail a discount for your clothes and have a chance to pay30 to 50% less. If you are not bothered about wearing clothes that are in style then you can get up to 50% off on the previous season's clothing. You can look for coupon codes on websites that give them away and use them on the site where you wish to purchase your items. Make sure you buy in bulk again and not buy anymore for a long time.

Service gift

It is possible to save on a few hundred dollars by deciding to gift a service to someone. This means that you not give away a physical gift and instead settle for a service. You can trim their lawn, help clean their bedroom, cook a meal for them, baby sit their children or pets etc. As long as it adds value to their life, you can gift them any service that you like. But remember to fulfill the service and not refuse it as that might cause bad blood between the two of you.

Crock pot

You can save a lot on your electricity bills by making use of a crock pot. Unlike an oven or a hot plate, the crock pot cooks food at a low temperature and so, does not draw in too much electricity. You can buy a good crock pot and use it to cook all your food. All you have to do is add in all the ingredients and allow it to cook for 6 to 12 hours. You meals will be ready and you need not expend too much of your own energy in cooking your meals. You can buy a good quality crock pot from an online store.

Leftovers

It is advisable for you to make the best use of your leftovers. You can heat it up and eat it the next day for breakfast. If you stick leftovers in the fridge then you can use it for a couple of days to make fresh meals and can also carry it to office. You need to plan your meals for the entire week as it will help you stop wasting food. You can prepare everything on a Sunday and have it kept ready for you to simply toss everything into a crock pot and carry on with your other activities.

Raise!

It is never a bad idea to ask for a raise. If you work in a place that allows you to have a flexible pay system then don't be afraid to ask for a raise. Maybe your boss will be interested in giving you one but expecting you to ask first. Through hard work and determination, it is possible for you to get a raise often and the bonus that you attain can be directed towards repaying your loan amount.

Remember that these are just a few of the ways in which you can save money on a daily basis and there can be many more that you must surmise and adopt depending on your lifestyle.

Chapter 14

Investment Options For You

When you have a lot of debt to repay, you might want to consider using your saved up money to invest in places that will double or even triple it in value. This will help you in using the excess to repay debt and possibly be left with some extra money for yourself.

But your investments need to be short term as you need to repay your loans at the earliest and not drag it for 10 or 12 years. In this chapter, we will look at some of the best short term investments that you can choose to invest your money in and use the money to repay your debts.

Short term investments options

Before we begin, you must understand that even the short term investments can take anywhere from a year to 3 years to grow in value and so, you must remain patient with it. Once they mature or grow in value, you can deal with them according to your plan and use the surplus to repay your debts.

Bank deposits

The easiest and most preferred short term investment that people use is bank savings. Banks will take your money and return it to you with an interest. What this does is, helps you increase the value of your savings. Say for example you have 3000$ debt and 2500$ savings. You can put this savings into a bank and make it 3000$ in say a year and repay all your debt. This will ensure that you close out the debt at once and do not have to rely on the installment method. But remember to choose a good bank that offers a high rate of interest and compounds interest on a yearly basis as opposed to half or quarterly. You must also choose an account that pays more interest than the others.

Certificate deposits

Certificate deposits are government schemes where you purchase a bond or certificate for a certain amount of money that is much lesser than its face value. When you sell these bonds, the government will pay its face value, which will be much higher than what you paid for it. So this type of investment will be a great option for you if you wish to choose the snowballing method to repay your debts. You can avail a bond for 3 months, 6 months or a year depending on when you wish for it to mature.

Mutual funds

Ultra short term mutual funds or debt funds are great options for you when you wish to make short term investments. These are meant to give away profits within a year to 3 years of investing. You can possibly double you amount if you choose the right type of company to invest in. you might have to consult someone who has a good knowledge on the subject and seek their opinion on the best company to invest in. once you make your choice take it up seriously and invest your money at the earliest.

Commodities

The commodities market is a great place to invest for short term purposes. All you have to do is invest your money in a commodity of your choice and it can range between potatoes, onions, sugar and other such commodities. As soon as the price of these commodities rises, you will have a chance to make a profit and this surplus can be used to repay your debt. The commodities market can fluctuate quite a lot but when the time is right, selling your shares will help you make quite a substantial amount of money.

Business investments

Investing in business that will have a quick rate of turnover can make for great short term investments. All you have to do is invest money in a business that looks promising and wait for it to turn successful. Once the company makes it big, you will probably receive double of what you invested, or more, and you will not have to worry about your loan amount. But remember to do a thorough research before you invest in a company and do so only if you are fully confident of earning back a good sum of money.

Gold

Gold and precious stones are good investments and they can grow in value in no time. You can buy them when they are low and then sell them when their prices rise. This will help you make a profit and use the money to repay your debts.

These are the best short term investment options that you can consider and hope you make the right choice for yourself.

Key Highlights

Now, let us look at some of the key highlights of this book. There were many things that were discussed and you need to look at them again just to be reminded of the key take aways from this book.

- Remember that debt repayment is an important part of life. It is not something that can be taken lightly and you need to put in as much effort as required to pay off all your debts at the earliest. With your debts paid off and having enough money saved up, you will have a chance to retire early and live a happy life. You will not have to worry about your family and they will have a great life if you pay off all your debt

- You need to be organized in order to make the most of your resources. If you remain disorganized then you will not know how much money you have and how much is getting used up. For this, you need to make use of lists. Use your lists to understand how much income you have and how much expenses you need to take care of. Once you make a list of both, you will have an idea of the amount of money that you are left with. You will have a chance to rework your expenses and increase your income

- Remember that you have to prepare the list in an orderly way. You need to set yourself a particular place and be there on time to finish it. You might have to make use of your computer and come up with a list that is fool proof and accurate. Don't think of this process as mundane or trivial and give it top most priority

- You can rework your expenses in such a way that it matches your income or is lesser than what you make on a monthly basis. If you don't do so, then you will find it tough to repay your debt and save money for your future. Living from paycheck to paycheck is not advisable as you might run out of money and not have enough to pay off your debts. You need to plan your way out of it and cannot simply expect it to work for you. once you rework your expenses and boot out the unnecessary ones, you will have a chance to save more money on a monthly basis

- You can make use of your skills to increase your monthly income. This can be done through side jobs or by indulging in sales. You can take up a side job of your choice and try and make as much money from it as possible and contribute some towards debt repayment and some towards savings. You must try and make the most of your spare time and instead of whiling it away, you can put it to good use by taking up a hobby and making money out of it

- Many people don't think it is wise to save when there is a lot of debt but this is only a misconception. It is never a bad idea to save money and you must do so as and when an opportunity presents itself. You must make it a point to not waste a single penny and contribute it towards your savings. You never know when you might require some extra cash and once you have savings, you can put it to good use. So don't take savings lightly and try and save as much as possible for a brighter future

- You can repay your debt in any which way that you like. Some prefer the snowballing effect while others like to do it the other way round. Depending on the amount that you have saved up to repay your debts, you can choose the type of method. But once you start repaying you must not stop until everything is fully paid for. You must maintain a consistent record mentioning your debts and also how much has been paid for and how much remains

- Remember that you have to live within a budget for as long as required. A budget is used to help you curb unnecessary spending and not meant to wreak havoc in your life. Think of it as a life saver and use it to rescue yourself from debt. You cannot live a life where the stress of debt hounds you. You need to breathe and live freely and for that, you must give up on small pleasures and look at the bigger picture. Once you are done with your debts, you can live a happy life

- Remember that your credit cards are your existing debt's worst enemies. They will only add to your debts and slow you down. So decide to do away with as many cards as you can and try and have just one, which you can use occasionally. Using cash is the best option for you and you will have a lot more control over your money without the fear of inviting interest. So modify your purchasing techniques and carry cash with you whenever you step out to buy something

- If you make use of your business mind and invest your savings into a short term scheme, you will have enough money to repay your debts and also have some surplus to fund an ornate lifestyle

Conclusion

Hopefully, this book has given you a lot of help and insight on how to be debt-free and how to achieve financial freedom. Read it once, twice, or even more, and keep going back to it until you have learned it by heart. It is not only meant to tell you what to do, but it is also aimed at inspiring you to continue living a life of financial comfort, happiness, and satisfaction.

Feel free to develop or modify the lists, charts, methods, and tips that you learned in this book, as long as it matches your own values and what makes you feel right. Remember that everybody plans differently for their financial freedom and you need to do what you think is right. Don't copy someone else's plans and come up with your very own.

Commit to paying off your credit card/consumer debt using the payment process you learned. It is the most effective payment process that there is to get you out of debt as soon as possible.

Good luck, and may you find yourself debt-free and financially free much sooner than you expect!

Finally, if you enjoyed this book, then I'd like to ask you for a favor, would you be kind enough to leave a review for this book on Amazon? It'd be greatly appreciated!

Thank you,

Richard

Check Out My Other Books

Below you'll find some of my other books that are popular on Amazon and Kindle as well.

Personal Finance: 7 Steps To Effective Budgeting and Money Management To Build Personal Wealth

Credit Repair: How To Repair Credit And Remove ALL Negative Items From Your Credit Report Forever

www.ingramcontent.com/pod-product-compliance
Lightning Source LLC
Chambersburg PA
CBHW070846180526
45168CB00002B/972